Contents

Is the government important to the economy?   4

Has the government's role in the economy changed?   8

How does the government raise money?   14

Where else does the government get money?   18

What does the government do with our money?   22

Does the government spend money overseas?   30

How does the government keep the economy working?   32

Why does all this matter to me?   40

In focus: What are the world's strangest taxes?   42

Money facts   44

Glossary   46

Find out more   47

Index   48

You can find the answers to the Solve it! questions on page 45.

Some words are shown in bold, **like this**. You can find out what they mean by looking in the glossary on page 46.

Is the government important to the economy?

If you watch the news, read newspapers, or click onto news websites you will see lots of news about the **economy**, and it may all seem very confusing.

The basic parts of the economy are not too complicated. We all buy and consume things, meaning we are all **consumers**. Most adults work to earn money and make the things consumers need. Business owners, or **capitalists**, own the businesses and pay the workers. They **invest** money to make more money, or **profit**.

These people are going to work on a train. Their work will create wealth and they will be paid money, which they will spend on things for themselves and their families.

Understanding Money

Money and Government

Nick Hunter

www.raintreepublishers.co.uk
Visit our website to find out
more information about
Raintree books.

To order:
☎ Phone 0845 6044371
🖹 Fax +44 (0) 1865 312263
🖳 Email myorders@raintreepublishers.co.uk

Customers from outside the UK please telephone +44 1865 312262

Raintree is an imprint of Capstone Global Library Limited,
a company incorporated in England and Wales having its
registered office at 7 Pilgrim Street, London, EC4V 6LB –
Registered company number: 6695582

Edited by Megan Cotugno
Designed by Ryan Frieson
Original illustrations © Capstone Global Library, Ltd.
Illustrated by Planman Technologies
Picture research by Mica Brancic
Originated by Capstone Global Library, Ltd.
Printed and bound in China by Leo Paper Products Ltd.

ISBN 978 1 4062 2171 8 (hardback)
15 14 13 12 11
10 9 8 7 6 5 4 3 2 1

ISBN 978 1 4062 2178 7 (paperback)
16 15 14 13 12
10 9 8 7 6 5 4 3 2 1

British Library Cataloguing in Publication Data
Hunter, Nick.
 Money and government. -- (Understanding money)
 1. Economic policy--Juvenile literature.
 I. Title II. Series
 338.9-dc22

Acknowledgements
We would like to thank the following for permission to
reproduce photographs:

Alamy p. 41 (© Shoosmith Collection); Corbis pp. 4 (© Tim
Pannel), 8 (© Bettmann), 9 (© Stapleton Collection/Philip
Spruyt ca. 2003), 16 (© Daniel Hambury/epa November 08,
2007), 19 (© Hulton-Deutsch Collection), 21 (© Stephen Hird/
Reuters), 42 (© Bettmann), 25 (© Randy Faris), 26 (© Roy
Rainford), 31 (© Patrick Chauvel), 32 (© Charles O'Rear), 33
(© Louie Psihoyos/Science Faction), 35 (© Geray Sweeney),
37 (© ANDY RAIN/epa), 38 (© Image Source), 39 (© Alessia
Pierdomenico/Reuters); Getty Images p. 13 (Hulton Archive),
15 (Matt Cardy); iStockphoto p.43 (© Christian Sanzey); Mary
Evans Picture Library p. 10 (Peter Higginbotham Collection);
Photoshot p. 7 (UPPA/Mark Fairhurst); Shutterstock pp. 5 (©
alessandro0770), 12 (© Adrian Reynolds), 29 (© Brasiliao), 17
(© Iofoto)

Cover photo of Bank of England, London reproduced with
permission of Shutterstock (© Christopher Walker).

Every effort has been made to contact copyright holders of
material reproduced in this book. Any omissions will be
rectified in subsequent printings if notice is given to the
publishers.

All the Internet addresses (URLs) given in this book were valid
at the time of going to press. However, due to the dynamic
nature of the Internet, some addresses may have changed, or
sites may have changed or ceased to exist since publication.
While the author and Publishers regret any inconvenience this
may cause readers, no responsibility for any such changes can
be accepted by either the author or the Publishers.

The Houses of **Parliament** in London are where the government makes laws for the UK. Many of these laws are about money and the economy.

Creating wealth

The workers and the business owners create **wealth**. Wealth does not just mean money. It means things that are made by human work. Most things we use or need are created by work. Food is grown and then prepared for us to eat. Factories make goods like TVs and computers. An economy is the total of all the wealth created in a society.

The world economy includes all the wealth created in the world. The economy of our own country is linked to the world economy in lots of ways. The government of our country has a very important role to play. This book will look at where the government's money comes from and how it uses money.

In most countries, the people vote to decide who will be in charge of the country. This is called **democracy**. **Politicians** who want to be elected make promises about what money they will spend on things like hospitals and schools. The group of politicians who gets the most votes becomes the government.

Raising and spending money

Before the government can spend any money, it needs to raise money. Everyone in the country has to give the government some money. This is called tax. Politicians make promises about how much tax people will pay if they are elected to be the government.

The government uses the money from taxes to pay for many of the **services** we use every day, such as the road outside your house. More people work for the government than for anyone else.

Apart from raising taxes and spending money, the government also has to make sure that the economy runs smoothly. The government passes laws to protect consumers, workers, and business owners. A bit like a referee in a football match, the government needs to make sure that the rules of the economy are obeyed and that all parts of the economy work properly.

How much does the government spend?

In 2009–2010, the UK government expected to spend around £10,000 for each person in the country on everything from schools to the army. More than £4 of every £10 spent in the country is spent by the government.

If the government cannot raise enough money in taxes, they may have to cut some services. These people are protesting about cuts to the health service.

Has the government's role in the economy changed?

Ever since the first states organized themselves, governments have always wanted to tax people. More than 4,000 years ago, in Ancient Egypt, records made by **scribes** show that some of the grain that was grown each year would go to the royal granaries as a tax.

Tax was also one of the causes of the English Civil War, which began in 1640. King Charles I tried to impose taxes without the agreement of Parliament.

In ancient civilizations, taxes were much less important than they are now as governments did not need to spend as much money. Fighting wars was usually the biggest expense for governments. Ancient Greek states would collect special taxes to pay for wars. Tax became more important in the Roman Empire because of the cost of the Roman armies. Taxes on property and goods developed through the medieval period.

Unpopular taxes

Throughout history, people have disliked paying taxes. Tax has been a cause of many conflicts between governments and ordinary people. "No taxation without representation" became a popular cry among Americans who wanted **independence** from Britain in the 1770s. They believed that, as they could not vote for the British government, they should not have to pay tax to it.

Like tax itself, tax collectors have been unpopular throughout history.

"In this world nothing can be said to be certain, except death and taxes."

Benjamin Franklin, American statesman, 1789

9

Victorian workhouses were designed to be as unpleasant as possible, to stop people claiming help unless they really needed it.

Governments have often spent more on war than anything else. The first **income tax** on the money people earn was started in Britain in 1799 to pay for a war against France. The world wars of the 20th century were very expensive and new taxes were put in place to pay for them.

Public spending

In the 1800s, many of the things that the government spends money on today did not exist. Services that are now paid for by government were provided by local **parishes** or private charities. If we get ill, we can go and see a doctor. In the 1800s, this was only possible if you could pay the doctor. Those who were unemployed or too old to earn money had to rely on their families. If they could not get help anywhere else, they had to go into a **workhouse**, where only very basic food and shelter was provided. Health care, education, and other **benefits** are now provided in the UK and some other countries, but many countries still do not provide these services.

The welfare state

At the end of World War Two, a new government promised to introduce a system of social benefits that would look after the people of Britain "from the cradle to the grave". The National Health Service would provide health care for everyone. Systems of old age **pensions**, **unemployment**, and sickness benefits would be expanded. However, this meant that the government had to spend more than before on health and welfare.

Making money

To run smoothly, the **economy** needs a supply of money. Governments are responsible for making the money that we use. In most cases this is managed by a central **bank** like the Bank of England, which was set up in 1694.

The government also has to protect the **rights** of businesses, workers, and **consumers**. In the 1700s, during the Industrial Revolution, many people moved to the cities and started working in factories. Factory owners often **employed** children, because they could pay them less money. Governments passed laws that stopped this. They also put limits on the number of hours that people could be made to work, and improved working conditions.

In recent years, lots of laws have been passed to protect the rights of consumers. For example, products that might be dangerous to health must carry warnings or may be banned.

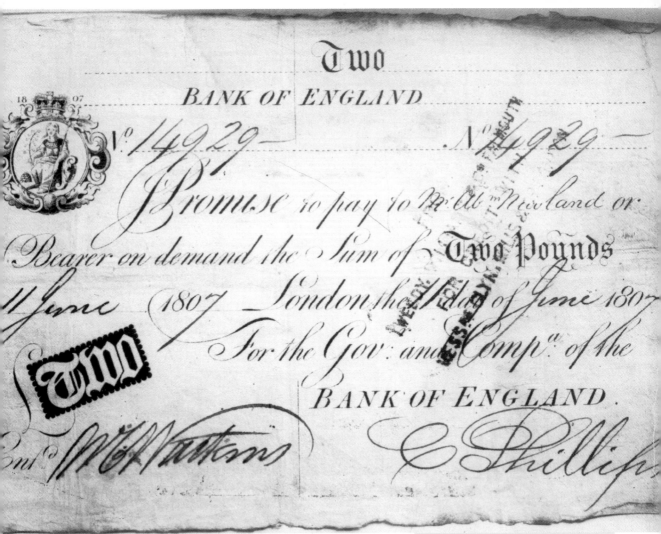

The banking crisis of 2008

Banks are an important part of the economy. People put money in banks to keep it safe. Banks then lend this money to other people and businesses. In 2008, there were problems in the banking system and people worried that their savings might not be safe. The government stepped in to support the banks.

The earliest banknotes were handwritten and signed by the Chief Cashier of the Bank of England. The first fully printed notes came into use in England and Wales in 1855.

How does the government raise money?

The main way that the government raises money is through taxes. We pay taxes in many different ways.

Direct taxes

Direct taxes are those that are paid directly by individuals. **Income tax** is a direct tax as it is based on what someone earns. Most people who have a job will have income tax taken from their pay. Those who earn more money will pay a higher tax rate. This means that they pay a higher proportion of their earnings in income tax.

In the UK, people who do paid work also have to pay **National Insurance**. This is calculated in a similar way to income tax as a part of what you earn. Companies also have to pay National Insurance for all their employees. National Insurance is supposed to pay for specific **services**, including health and old age **pensions**.

Other direct taxes are charged on particular items, normally affecting wealthier people. These include taxes on buying and selling land and houses. Businesses also have to pay tax on the money they make.

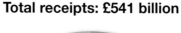

Total receipts: £541 billion

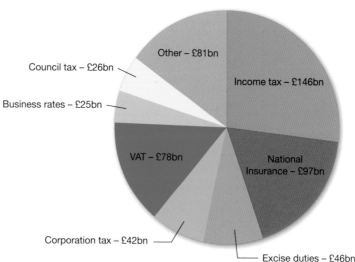

Other – £81bn
Council tax – £26bn
Business rates – £25bn
Income tax – £146bn
VAT – £78bn
National Insurance – £97bn
Corporation tax – £42bn
Excise duties – £46bn

This chart shows the main ways in which the UK government raises money.

Source: HM Treasury, 2010-11 estimates. Other receipts include capital taxes, stamp duties, vehicle excise duties and some other tax and non-tax receipts- for example, interest and dividends. Figures may not sum to total due to rounding

The Chancellor of the Exchequer

Each year, the British government's **Budget** is presented by the Chancellor of the Exchequer. The Chancellor is the government minister responsible for the **economy**. He or she decides how much money the government needs to raise and how to raise it. The Chancellor then explains these plans in the Budget speech to the **House of Commons**. People listen to the Budget to find out if they will have to pay more taxes in future.

Indirect taxes

Everyone who spends money pays tax. We pay taxes every time we buy something in a shop, make a phone call or almost any way you can think of to spend money. Value Added Tax (VAT) is a proportion of the cost of everything that gets passed to the government.

This is an indirect tax as we do not pay the tax direct to the government when we buy something. It is normally included in the price we pay so we don't notice it in the same way as a direct tax. The tax is then paid to the government by the shop or business.

VAT is not the only indirect tax. **Excise duties** are special taxes on particular items. They are often designed to change people's behaviour. For example, excise duties are charged on alcohol and tobacco products. These products cost more to buy. The government hopes this will encourage people to live healthier lives by reducing the amount they drink and smoke.

Excise duty is charged on fuel for vehicles. This is designed to make driving expensive so people use their cars less. Many people believe this is unfair because in some places people have no alternative to driving to work or school.

These girls will pay a tax on the items they buy from this shop.

Solve it!

Direct or indirect taxes?

This chapter has looked at how the government raises tax. Which taxes do you think are fairer? Direct taxes normally mean that wealthier people pay more. Do indirect taxes like VAT mean that we all pay our fair share? What do you think?

Where else does the government get money?

Sometimes the government needs to spend more than it can get from taxes. If the government is spending more than it earns, this is called a **deficit**. If the government needs more money, it can borrow money by selling a bond.

A bond is a promise to pay back the money after a certain amount of time. Ordinary people and businesses like **banks** can buy bonds and this money goes to the government. The government will also pay some money every year, called **interest**, to the person who bought the bond.

How bonds work

If I buy a bond for £100 that is due to be repaid in three years, the government pays me interest of perhaps 5p for every pound I borrowed. If we multiply that 5p by 100, we find that the government will pay me £5 every year. After three years I will get my original £100 back, in addition to the interest I have earned (£5 x 3 years = £15).

The National Debt

The total amount of money that the British government has borrowed in bonds is called the National Debt. In 2010, the total debt was £848.5 billion. This is about 60 per cent of the size of everything bought and sold in the UK **economy** in 2010 (called **Gross Domestic Product** or GDP). The government pays many billions of pounds of interest for the National Debt every year.

The National Debt rises in wartime. These people are celebrating the end of World War Two. At that time, the UK's National Debt was almost twice as much as GDP.

Local government

Not all taxes go to central government. Local **councils** in cities, counties, and towns also need money. Local councils have to pay for **services** such as rubbish collection, police, schools, and roads. Some of the money spent by local government is paid to them by central government. However, they also need to raise money from local people.

Local councils in the UK raise money through council tax. This is paid by each household in the local area. The amount of council tax that people pay depends on the **value** of their house. The bigger your house, the more council tax you have to pay. Businesses like shops and restaurants also have to pay a tax for local services, called a business rate.

Other parliaments

Scotland, Wales, and Northern Ireland have their own governments. However, people who live there still pay taxes to the UK government in London. A portion of those taxes is then passed back to Scotland, Wales, and Northern Ireland so the local **parliaments** can decide how to spend it.

Protesting about tax

In the late 1980s, the government tried to introduce a tax called the community charge to pay for local services. It became known as the poll tax. Each person had to pay the same amount, no matter how much money they had. Many people felt this was unfair and protested against the tax. It was replaced with the council tax.

Firefighters to keep us safe are just one of the essential local services that councils have to pay for.

What does the government do with our money?

You will often hear people complaining about how much tax they have to pay. We have already seen that almost every time we earn or spend money, it is taxed. However, governments do not just tax people for the sake of it. They tax us because they need the money to govern the country and provide **services**.

People also argue about how the government spends our money. Some people think that more should be spent on health or education. Others think that the government should spend less and that more services should be provided by businesses instead. This chapter will look at the main services the government spends money on, and why we need those services.

The big three

The biggest areas of government spending are:

- Social protection, including old age **pensions** and **benefits** for people who are unemployed

- Health

- Education, including schools, colleges, and universities.

There are lots of areas which cost less than these three, such as building roads, police, and prisons. Even the smallest section of the pie chart (**industry**, agriculture, and employment) still costs over £300 per year for every person in the country.

Total managed expenditure: £704 billion

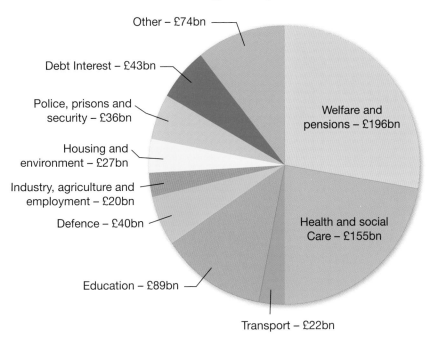

Other – £74bn

Debt Interest – £43bn

Police, prisons and security – £36bn

Housing and environment – £27bn

Industry, agriculture and employment – £20bn

Defence – £40bn

Education – £89bn

Transport – £22bn

Welfare and pensions – £196bn

Health and social Care – £155bn

Government spending changes every year. In 2010, the new government said they would cut spending in many areas.

Source: HM Treasury 2010-11 near-cash projections. The allocation of spending to functions is largely based on the United Nations' classifications of the functions of Government (COFOG). Other expenditure includes general public services (including international services); recreation, culture, and religion; public service pensions; plus spending yet to be allocated and some accounting adjustments. Social protection includes tax credit payments in excess of an individual's tax liability, which are now counted in AME, in line with OECD guidelines. Figures may not sum due to rounding.

Where does the money go?

This pie chart shows the things that government spends money on. You can see that each section of the chart is bigger or smaller depending on how much is spent. The different sections add up to the government's whole **budget**. Try putting together a pie chart for what you spend your pocket money on. Which will be the biggest sections?

Keeping us healthy

Health care is an essential service we all use. The National Health Service (NHS) was at the centre of the plan for the welfare state in 1946. Spending on health includes hospitals and ambulances, but also everyday medical care such as local GPs. Around 17p of every £1 the UK government spends is used for health care.

Many European countries have a health service that patients do not have to pay for directly. In the United States and many other countries people have to pay for health **insurance** so that when they are ill, insurance companies will cover part of the costs of medical treatment.

There is often a lot of political debate about the NHS. This is partly because so much government money is spent on it, but also because people's health is so important. Some people believe that lots of money is wasted by the government and that health care would be more efficient if it was provided by private companies.

Why is so much spent on health care?

One of the reasons why so much money is spent on health care is the number of people who are paid by the government. More than 1,500,000 people work for the NHS, including doctors and nurses, but also cooks, cleaners, and everyone needed to run the health care system. The cost of drugs and equipment needed to treat illnesses also rises every year.

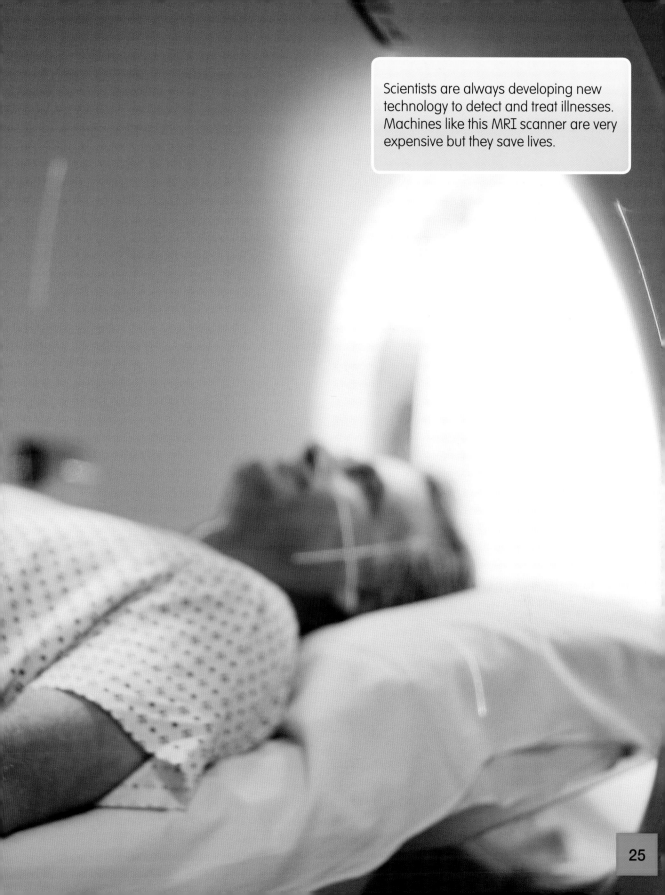

Scientists are always developing new technology to detect and treat illnesses. Machines like this MRI scanner are very expensive but they save lives.

Price of an education

In 2009, UK state schools cost £5,660 per student every year. If a student stays at school for 12 years and costs stay the same as in 2009, their education will cost the government nearly £68,000.

Universities like Cambridge attract students from around the world. Foreign students pay more than UK students because some of the cost for UK students is paid by the government.

Education

Education is another area that is a priority for government spending. Parents want their children to have the best education possible. A good education system is also good for the country. Companies who are looking for skilled workers are more likely to **employ** people in countries with a strong education system. Many **developing countries** have put lots of money into education as they believe this will help their economies.

Most of the education budget goes to schools. Some of this money comes directly from central government and some comes through local authorities. At any time, there are about 8,000,000 students in UK schools. Think about all the things that have to be paid for in your school: your teachers' wages, heating and lighting, books, computers, and all the other things that help you to learn.

Universities and colleges

The other main area of education spending is on education after you leave school. Unlike most schools, students often have to pay to go to university. Spending money for universities is often not such a priority for government as spending money on schools. Schools benefit everyone, but not everyone goes to college or university.

Welfare and benefits

As we saw earlier in this chapter, the biggest cost for governments is social welfare. Protecting people who are not able to earn money is one of the main roles of modern government. The cost of welfare and benefits has grown enormously in the last century.

Old age pensions were first introduced in the UK in 1908. The government pays money to everyone over a certain age so they do not have to do paid work. Before 1908, people had to rely on their families to look after them if they were too old to work. Many people also save some money while they are working so they will have enough money to live on when they **retire**. The government also provides benefits for people who are unable to work for other reasons, such as illness or disability.

Solve it!

Pension problem

People are living longer than they have in the past. This is because doctors can cure more illnesses and people are living healthier lives. This will mean that old-age pension costs could increase. Why might this happen and what can the government do about it?

Benefit questions

Although most people agree that governments should pay welfare benefits to people who are unable to work, benefits are also controversial. Some people argue that the government pays benefits to too many people. They say that some people who receive money from the government do not feel they have to find work. Other people argue that it is difficult to get the right balance between supporting people who cannot earn money and helping them to find work.

Unemployment

Sometimes, even people who are able to work lose their jobs. They become unemployed. Government benefits help people when they lose their jobs and there are schemes to train them to do new jobs.

People lose their jobs for lots of reasons. Sometimes, things can be made more cheaply in other countries so UK factories have to close.

Does the government spend money overseas?

We have seen how government spending is used to provide **services** for ordinary people. The government also has to protect the country from outside threats. These threats may come from other countries or **terrorists**. The government spends money on the army, navy, and air force through the Ministry of Defence.

Fighting wars

In the past, wars were one of the main costs of government. Many of the taxes we pay today were started to pay for wars. Although other areas of spending have grown, defence is still very expensive. Military equipment is costly and needs to be of the best quality when lives are at risk.

Many people think that all war is wrong. Others think that some wars, such as invasion of Iraq in 2003, should not be fought. People can protest about these wars, but they do not always have a choice about where the taxes they pay are spent. If we don't like the way the government spends our taxes, we can **vote** for someone else at the next **election**.

Tackling poverty

Around the world, about 1.4 billion people live on less than 80p (about $1.25) each day. These people do not have the health care and other support that we **benefit** from. Some of the money the government spends goes to support people living in poverty around the world. This money goes to long-term projects to improve people's lives. Some also goes to help with dealing with disasters such as earthquakes, floods, and **famine**.

Recent wars in Iraq and Afghanistan have meant that spending on defence has increased.

How does the government keep the economy working?

The role of the government in the **economy** is not just about taxing and spending money. The government is responsible for money itself.

The first money was made into coins of precious metals like gold and silver. The **value** of these coins was based on the actual weight of gold or silver in them. When banknotes were first used, they were linked directly to gold held by the **bank**. In England and Wales, banknotes are issued by the Bank of England. In Scotland and Northern Ireland, they can be issued by a number of banks.

Nowadays, a £10 note does not have any value in itself – it's just a piece of paper. We can only use it as money because the government and the bank that issued it promise that it is worth £10.

British banknotes are printed on paper. In some countries, such as Australia, banknotes are printed on plastic.

Printing money

Although a banknote is just a piece of paper, the
central bank need to make sure that people tr...
real. All banknotes issued by the Bank of Engl...
and other marks to show that they are genuin...
are always looking out for fake banknotes. Bar...
out. Old notes are collected by banks and repl...

Earlier we saw that if the govern...
money through taxes, it has...
bonds (see page 18). If th...
why doesn't it just prin...
needs to be careful...
much money is...
up. There wil...
because...
done...
ab...

Although the value of money
is no longer directly linked
to the value of gold, many
governments still keep gold
bars like this because the
value of gold is accepted by
all countries.

...ment cannot raise enough ...to borrow money by issuing ...e government needs more money, ...t more banknotes? The government ...how much money is printed. If too ...printed, there is a risk that prices will go ...be more money in the economy. However, ...the things being produced and the work being ...in the economy will not change, each banknote will be ...e to buy a bit less than before.

Inflation

If prices rise, this is called **inflation**. Some inflation is normal. You will notice that prices usually increase over time. If prices increase too fast this becomes a problem. Too much inflation means that money that people have saved is worth less. It can also mean that the money they earn will not buy as much as it did before. Governments try hard to control inflation.

The euro

If you've been abroad on holiday, you'll know that different money, or currency, is used in other countries. Until 2002, every country in Europe used a different currency. Now, if you travel to many European countries you will buy things in euros. These countries are members of the **European Union** (EU). Their governments decided to use the same currency. This makes it easier to travel to and **trade** with other countries in the EU. Some members of the EU, like the UK, have not switched to using the euro.

Shoppers in Dublin, Ireland, use the euro to pay for things.

Making laws

When a government is trying to get elected, **politicians** make lots of promises about what they will do when they win the **election**. Sometimes these promises are about how they are going to spend money. Often they are promising to pass laws that will help particular parts of the economy so that those people will **vote** for them.

Business owners are interested in laws that will make it easier for them to do business. This might mean providing new roads and airports for them to move goods and people. Business owners will also support laws that will save them money. Sometimes governments will provide money to support particular areas of business. This is called a **subsidy**.

Workers are more interested in laws that will protect their **rights**. The government sets a minimum wage, which is the lowest amount that workers can be paid. There are also laws about how long workers can be asked to work.

Paying for the government

The government also has to spend money on itself. All the **Members of Parliament** (MPs) who are elected and the many people who work with them need to be paid. MPs vote on how much they should pay themselves. Taxpayers watch this very closely to check that politicians are not spending too much money on themselves.

In 2009, newspapers discovered that many MPs had broken rules and used money from taxes to pay for things for themselves. One MP even used taxpayers' money to pay for a house for his ducks! Protestors floated a huge model of a duck house outside the Houses of Parliament.

E.CO.UK | DON'T DUCK CHANGE!

Protecting consumers

Advertisements are designed to make products look as good as possible so businesses can sell more. The government passes laws to protect **consumers**. Businesses need to make sure that anything they say about their products is true.

The government also makes laws about what products can be made from to ensure they will not cause any harm. Without these laws, businesses might try to make bigger **profits** by selling products that are unsafe or harmful.

Money in the bank

Most people keep the money they earn in the bank. Banks lend the money we save with them to other people and businesses. This system works fine as long as the banks do not lend too much and the people who borrow the money pay it back. The government and central banks watch the banks closely to make sure that people's savings are kept safe.

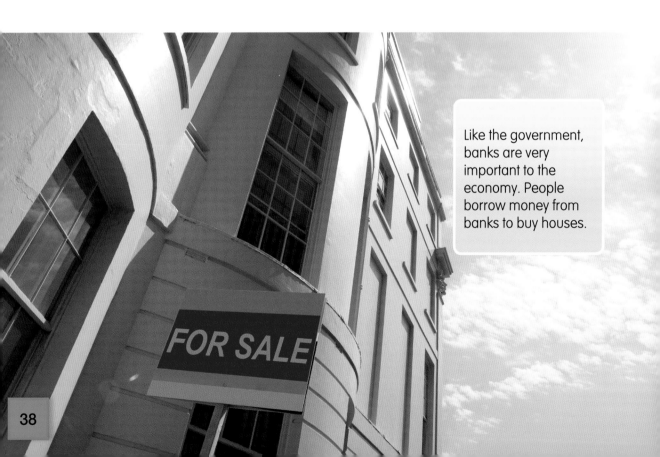

Like the government, banks are very important to the economy. People borrow money from banks to buy houses.

In 2007, people queued outside the Northern Rock bank. They wanted to take their money out of the bank because they were afraid that they might lose their savings.

If people did not trust the banks to look after their money, banks would have no money to lend. If banks cannot lend money then businesses will not be able to pay their workers and people will not be able to buy houses. In 2008, banks had made some bad choices about what to do with their money and many people did not trust them. The government had to give money to the banks and make sure that people's savings were safe.

Why does all this matter to me?

Hopefully this book will have helped you to understand why the government is such an important part of the **economy**. About £4 of every £10 spent in the UK economy is spent by the government, and we all pay taxes to fund this spending. Decisions made by the government affect all our lives.

It is important to understand how governments use your money. It may seem as if you couldn't possibly influence the decisions made by the government. Actually, we can influence what governments do. Anyone over the age of 18 can **vote** for or against the government in an **election**. Tax and government spending are always major issues that influence who people vote for. Even if you don't have a vote yet, you can complain to your local **council** or **MP**. For example, people often protest about decisions affecting local schools and hospitals.

What matters to you?

Think about which issues are important to you. Do you think that rich people should be taxed more than the rest of us? What do you think the government should spend more money on – schools, hospitals, or roads? What about local **services** like sports fields and parks? Decisions made by local and central government affect all of us and we can have a say in many of these decisions.

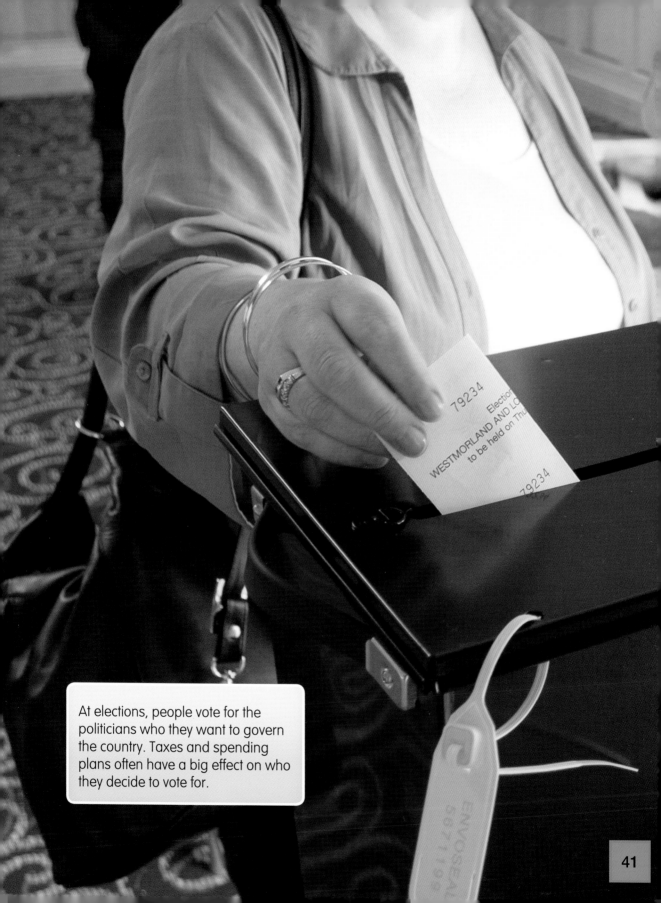

At elections, people vote for the politicians who they want to govern the country. Taxes and spending plans often have a big effect on who they decide to vote for.

IN FOCUS:

What are the world's strangest taxes?

Throughout history, governments have looked for new ways to tax people. Here are some of history's most unusual taxes.

Urine tax, ancient Rome

The Roman Emperor Vespasian (reigned CE 69–79) extended this tax to cover all the public toilets in Rome. Urine was used for making leather and dyeing cloth. Collectors would take the free urine from toilets and make money selling it.

Beard tax, Russia

Peter the Great (reigned 1682–1725) wanted Russia to become more like other European countries. He introduced this tax to encourage Russians to shave off their beards to look more like other Europeans of the time.

Window and hat taxes, Great Britain

Both these taxes were designed so that the wealthy would pay more tax. The window tax was introduced in 1696. People had to pay according to the number of windows in their houses. The hat tax was introduced in 1784. There were different levels depending on the type of hat.

Gas from cows, various countries

Many countries have considered taxing cows. A cow digesting its food produces more of the gases that cause global warming than most cars. A tax on cows would make beef more expensive. **Consumers** would eat less of it and that would reduce the number of cows.

Money facts

This chart shows the number of people who worked for the UK government at the end of 2009.

Industry	Number of people employed (000s)
Armed forces	198
Police	297
Public administration	1,208
Education	1,418
Health and social care	2,006
Other	970
Total public sector employment	6,097

Solve it!

Taxing question

On average, everyone in the UK pays about £10,000 in tax every year. Can you work out how much tax we would pay in each of the 12 months of the year? Using a calculator, can you work out how much we pay every day?

How much do governments spend in other countries?

Country	Central government spending (% of GDP)
Australia	34%
France	53%
Germany	43%
Ireland	42%
Japan	36%
Poland	43%
Spain	41%
Sweden	53%
UK	47%
USA	37%

*Source: OECD, figures for 2008 except *2007*

Answers to Solve it!

Page 29

Pension costs will go up because each person will be claiming a pension for more years. There will be more **retired** people and proportionately fewer people earning money.

Page 44

We would pay £833 tax per month, and £27.40 per day.

Glossary

bank business that takes money in from consumers and businesses and invests it by lending to other consumers and businesses

benefits can be any good or helpful outcome from an action. In the economy, it means extra things provided such as pensions.

budget amount of money to be used for a specific thing.

capitalist capitalism is an economic system that depends on people investing capital (money) to make and sell products. The people who invest money are capitalists.

consumer anyone who buys or uses the products made by capitalists. We are all consumers.

council group of people who meet regularly. Local areas are governed by local councils, who are elected.

currency money used in a country

deficit when a government spends more than it gets in tax, the difference between the two is called a deficit

democracy government voted for by the people they govern at an election

developing country poorer country where the economy is not yet fully developed, for example countries in Africa, Asia, and South America

economy total of all the wealth created in a society

elect vote for someone in an election

election process by which politicians or governments are elected

employ give someone a job, use their skill and time in return for payment

European Union group of countries in Europe that come together for trade and agree on many issues

excise duty tax on particular goods or products such as fuel

famine shortage of food

Gross Domestic Product (GDP) the total of everything bought and sold in an economy during any year. GDP is used to measure how big an economy is.

House of Commons building where Members of Parliament discuss and vote on new laws for the UK. New laws have to be agreed by the House of Commons.

income tax tax based on how much people earn

independence when a country or people wants to separate from their government and form a new one, they are said to want independence

industry area of the economy concerned with making raw materials into useful products, for example using metals in manufacturing

inflation process by which prices gradually go up over time

insurance agreement to reduce risks from accidents and other problems. People pay a regular amount every month and, in return, the insurance company will cover costs if an accident happens.

interest amount of money that is paid in return for money that is borrowed from a bank or lent to the government. If you save money in the bank, you will earn interest on that money.

invest use money in order to make a profit, for example by investing it in a business

Member of Parliament (MP) person who is elected to sit in the House of Commons

National Insurance tax paid by workers and businesses

parish area with its own church. In the past, churches and local councils were expected to look after the people in their parish

parliament the body that approves laws proposed by the government. In the UK, parliament is made up of the House of Commons and the House of Lords.

pension money that is paid to someone after they retire from working, either by the government or from money they have saved themselves

politician someone who is elected to local or national government

profit money that someone who invests money gets back on top of their initial investment

retire stop work, usually due to age

rights something that someone can claim they are entitled to, for example, the right to be paid for the work we do

scribe a person who copies out documents, especially one employed to do this before printing was invented

services public services are things like hospitals and schools provided by the government

subsidy money paid by the government to support a business, for example, subsidies might be paid to farmers to encourage them to grow certain crops

terrorist anyone who seeks to achieve political goals through violence

trade buying and selling, particularly buying and selling goods from other countries

unemployment being without a paid job

value how much something is worth

vote to support a politician in an election, usually by selecting them from a list of politicians

wealth anything that is produced by work. Wealth is also used to mean money.

workhouse institution for providing food and shelter for the poor, particularly during the 1800s

Find out more

Books

A Kid's Guide to the Economy, Tamara Orr, (Mitchell Lane Publishers, 2010)

Show Me the Money, Alvin Hall, (DK Publishing, 2008)

Websites

http://www.socialstudiesforkids.com/subjects/economics.htm
This website has information on basic economics, including supply and demand, scarcity, wants versus needs, and more.

https://www.cia.gov/library/publications/the-world-factbook/index.html
The CIA World Factbook has information and statistics about every country in the world.

Index

advertisements 38
Ancient Greece 9

banknotes 32, 33, 34
Bank of England 12,
  32, 33
banks 13, 18, 32, 33,
  38–39
behaviour 16, 43
bonds 18, 34
budget 15, 23, 26, 27,
  40
business owners. See
  capitalists.
business rates 20

capitalists 4, 5, 6, 12,
  14, 16, 18, 20, 22,|
  36, 38, 39
central banks 12, 33,
  38
Chancellor of the
  Exchequer 15
child employment 12
colleges 27
consumers 4, 6, 12,
  38, 43
cost per person 6, 22,
  26
council tax 20
cow tax 43
currency 32, 33, 34

deficits 18
democracy 6
developing countries 27
direct tax 14
disasters 30

economies 4, 5, 6, 12,
  13, 15, 18, 27, 32,

34, 36, 40
education 11, 22, 26,
  27
elections 6, 30, 36, 40
European Union (EU)
  34
excise duties 16

factories 5, 12

global warming 43
goods 5, 9, 36
Gross Domestic
  Product (GDP) 18

hat tax 43
House of Commons 15

income tax 11, 14
indirect tax 16
Industrial Revolution 12
inflation 34
interest 18
investments 4

laws 6, 12, 36, 38
loans 13, 38, 39
local governments 20,
  27, 40

Members of Parliament
  (MPs) 36, 40
military 30
minimum wage 36
Ministry of Defence 30

National Debt 18
National Health Service
  (NHS) 11, 24
National Insurance 14
Northern Ireland 20, 32

old-age pensions 11,
  14, 22, 28, 29

poll tax 20
poverty 30
profits 4, 38
protests 20, 30, 40

rights 12, 36
Roman Empire 9

savings 13, 28, 38, 39
Scotland 20, 32
services 6, 11, 14, 20,
  22, 24, 30, 40
social welfare 11, 14,
  22, 24, 28, 29
subsidies 36

taxes 6, 8–9, 11, 14,
  15, 16, 17, 18, 20, 22,
  30, 32, 34, 36, 40, 43

unemployment 11, 22,
  28, 29
universities 22, 26, 27

Value Added Tax (VAT)
  16

Wales 20, 32
wars 9, 11, 30
wealth 5, 14, 43
window tax 43
workers 4, 5, 6, 11, 12,
  14, 24, 27, 28, 36, 39
workhouses 10, 11
world economy 5
World War Two 11, 19